Time,
our most precious commodity.

The Persian Alphabet

We want to simplify your Persian learning journey as it is such a unique & enigmatic language. There are 32 official Persian letters. The letters change form depending on their position in a word or when they appear separate from other letters. For example, the letter <u>gh</u>ayn غ has four ways of being written depending on where it appears in any given word:

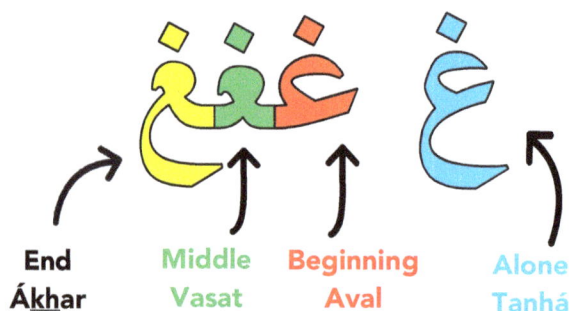

End	Middle	Beginning	Alone
Á<u>kh</u>ar	Vasat	Aval	Tanhá

It is important to note that Persian books are read from right to left (←). There are 7 separate/stand-alone letters that do not connect in the same way to adjacent letters (these will be depicted in blue). They are:

ا د ذ ر ز ژ و

Stand alone
Tanhá vámístan

The short vowels a, e & o are usually omitted in literature and are depicted by markings above & below letters (‗). They are not allocated a letter name, unlike their long vowel counterparts á: alef, í: ye & ú: váv (و ى آ).

Englisi	Farsi		Englisi	Farsi		Englisi	Farsi
A a	اَ اَ ا 'alef		M m	م ممم mím		Y y	ى ييى ye
Á á	آ ا ا 'alef		N n	ن ننن nún		Z z	ذ ذذ zál
B b	ب بيب Be		O o	اُ اُ ا 		Z z	ز زز ze
D d	د دد dál		P p	پ پپپ pe		Z z	ض ضضض zád
E e	اِ ِ 		Q q	ق ققق qáf		Z z	ظ ظظظ zá
F f	ف ففف fe		R r	ر رر re		**Ch** <u>ch</u>	چ چچچ che
G g	گ گگگ gáf		S s	س سسس sin		**Gh** gh	غ غغغ ghayn
H h	ه ههه he		S s	ص صصص sád		**Kh** kh	خ خخخ khe
H h	ح ححح he		S s	ث ثثث se		**Sh** <u>sh</u>	ش ششش shín
Í í	ى ييى ye		T t	ت تتت te		**Zh** <u>zh</u>	ژ ژژ zhe
J j	ج ججج jim		T t	ط ططط tá		,	ع ععع ayn
K k	ک ككك káf		Ú ú	و وو váv			
L l	ل للل lám		V v	و ووو váv			

Letter Guide©

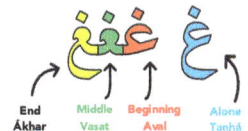

End Ákhar   Middle Vasat   Beginning Aval   Alone Tanhá

Pronunciation Guide©

Persian	English	Pronunciation
اَ	a	**a**nt
آ	á	**ar**m
ب	b	**b**at
د	d	**d**og
اِ	e	**e**nd
ف	f	**f**un
گ	g	**g**o
ه	h	**h**at
ح	h	**h**at
ی	í	m**ee**t
ج	j	**j**et
ک	k	**k**ey
ل	l	**l**ove
م	m	**m**e
ن	n	**n**ap
اُ	o	**o**n
پ	p	**p**at
ق	q/gh*	me**r**ci
ر	r	**r**un
س	s	**s**un
ص	s	**s**un
ث	s	**s**un

Persian	English	Pronunciation
ت	t	**t**op
ط	t	**t**op
و	ú	m**oo**n
و	v	**v**an
ی	y	**y**es
ذ	z	**z**oo
ز	z	**z**oo
ض	z	**z**oo
ظ	z	**z**oo
چ	ch	**ch**air
غ	gh*	me**r**ci
خ	kh*	ba**ch**
ش	sh	**sh**are
ژ	zh	plea**s**ure
ع	'	uh-oh†

*	: guttural sound from back of throat
†	: glottal stop, breathing pause
ّ	: Indicates a double letter
ً	: Indicates the letter n sound
لا	: Indicates combination of letter l & á (lá)
ای	: Indicates the long í sound (ee in m**ee**t)
ايِ	: Indicates the long í sound (ee in m**ee**t)
(...)	: Indicates colloquial use

Persian Numbers

A'dáde Fársí   عَدادِ فارسی

yek
پِک

do
دو

seh
سِه

chahár
چَهار

panj
پَنج

shesh
شِش

haft
هَفت

hasht
هَشت

noh
نُه

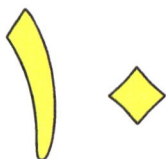

dah
دَه

yázdah
یازدَه

davázdah
دَوازدَه

to count

shemordan

شِمُر دَن

[to calculate: hesáb kardan]

á: as (a) in arm

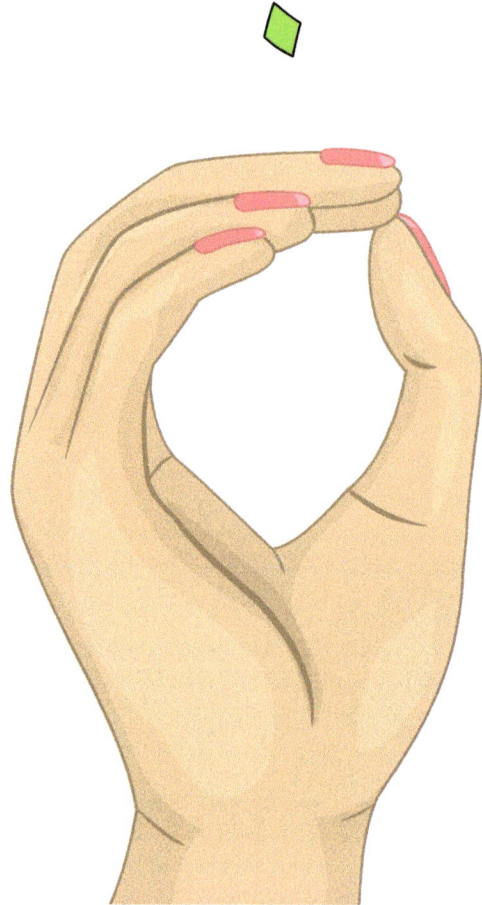

zero

sefr

صِفر

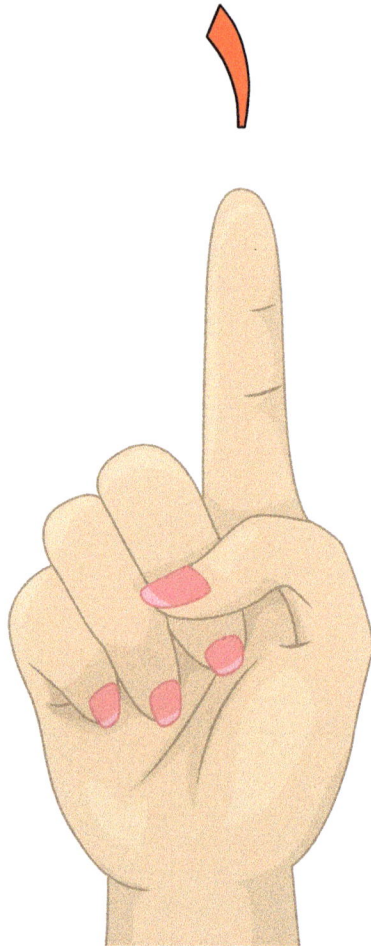

one

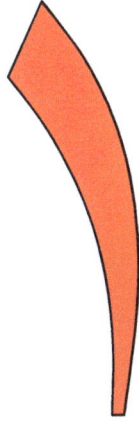

yek

پِک

١   ٢

two

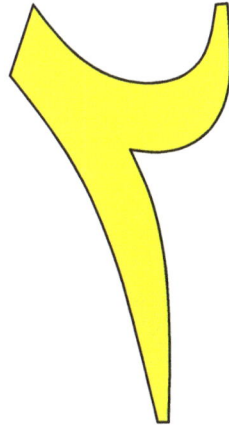

do

دو

١ ٢

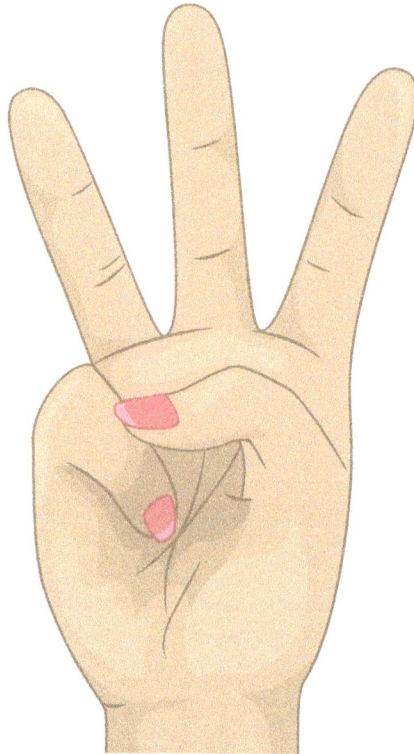

three

seh

سِه

۴ ۳ ۲ ۱

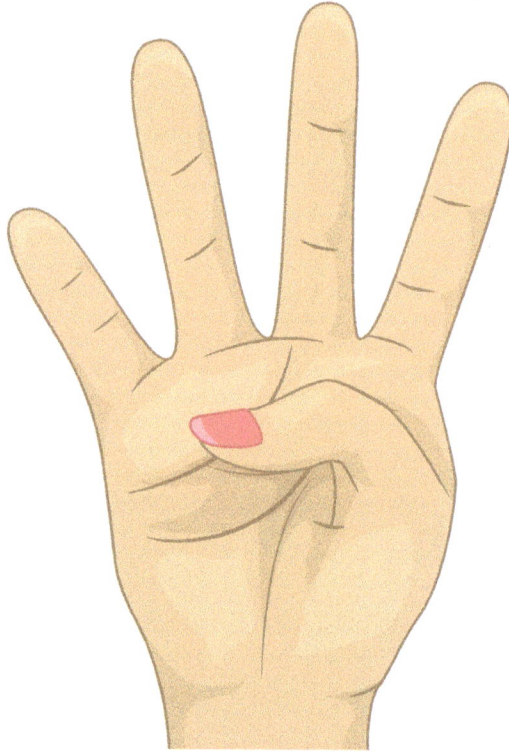

four

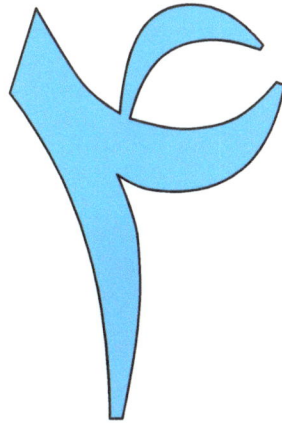

chahár

چَهار

á: as (a) in <u>a</u>rm

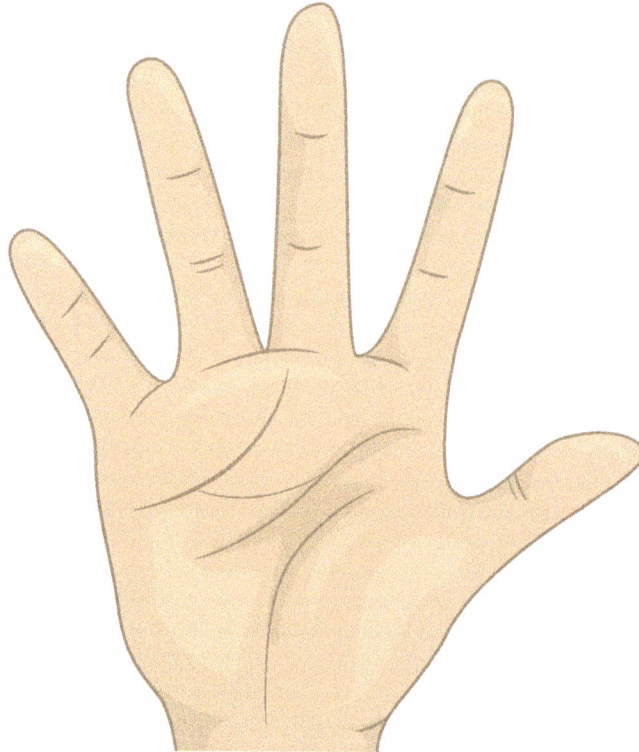

five

panj

پَنْج

۱

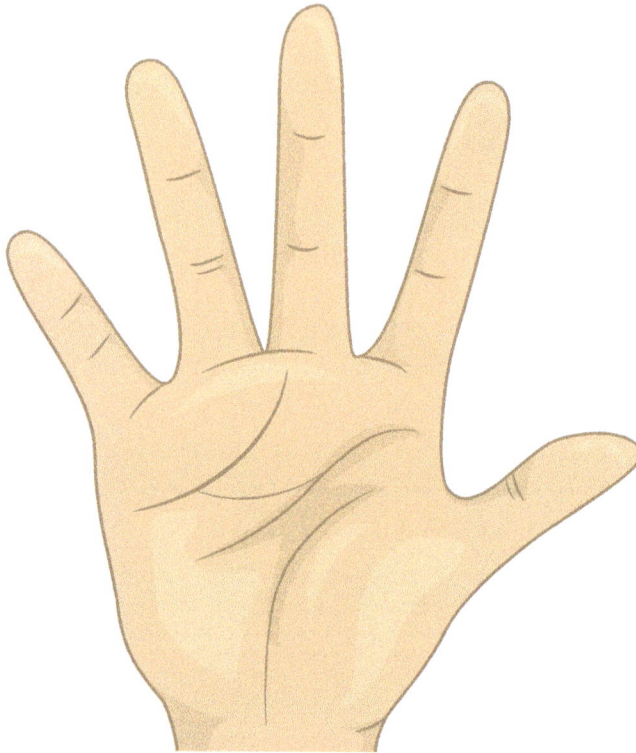 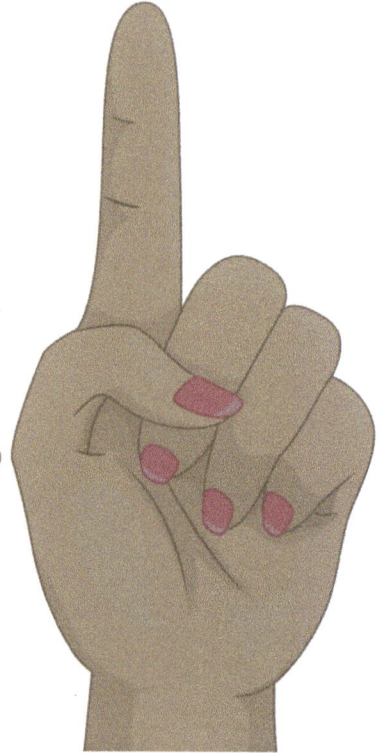

six

<u>sh</u>e<u>sh</u>

شِش

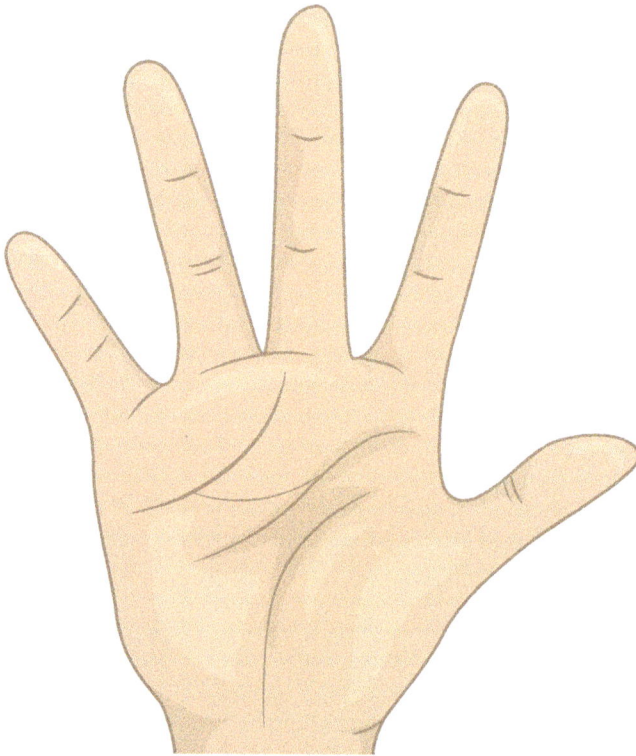 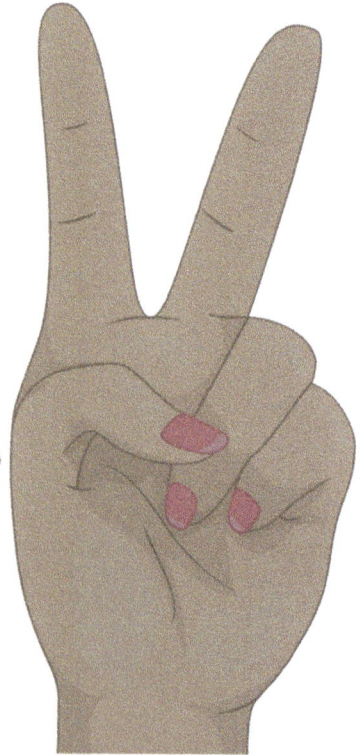

seven

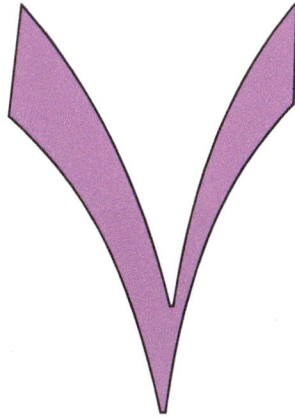

haft

هَفت

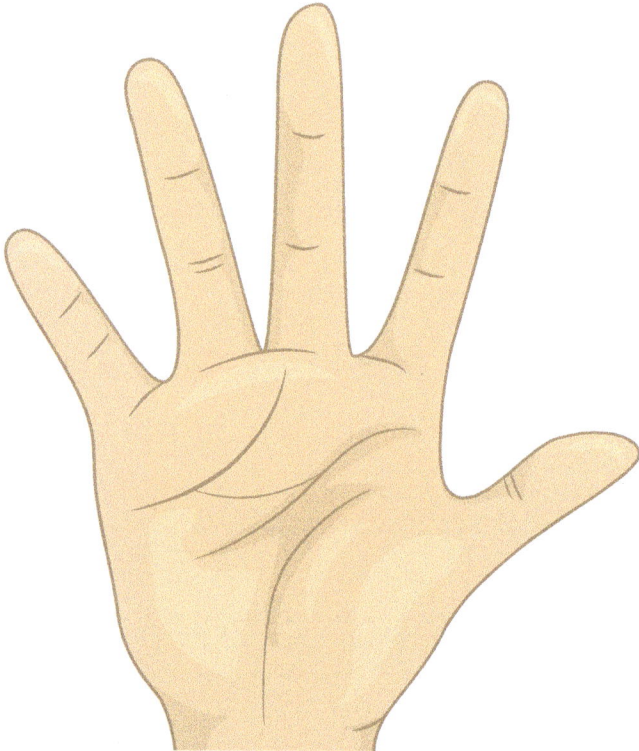

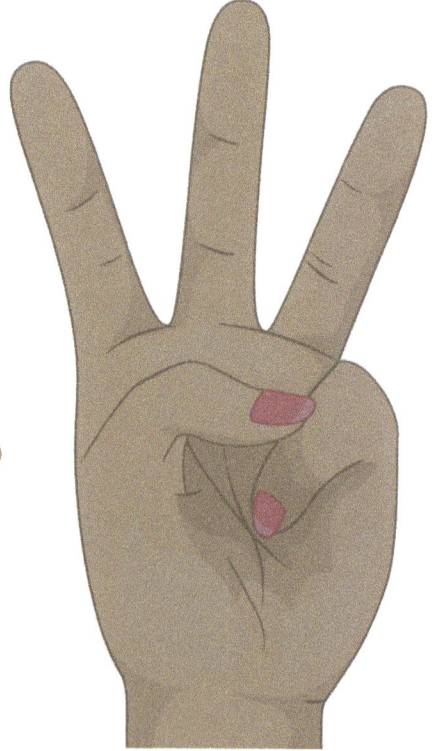

eight

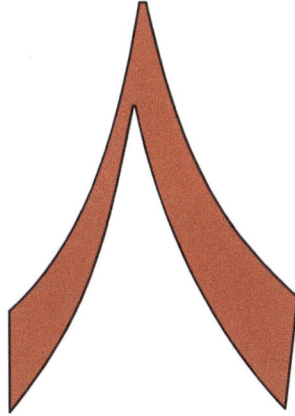

hasht

هَشت

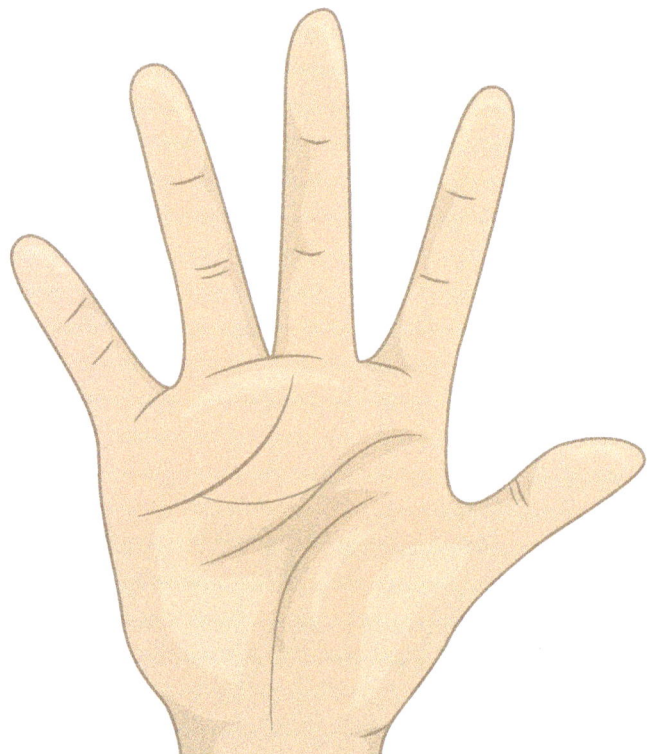 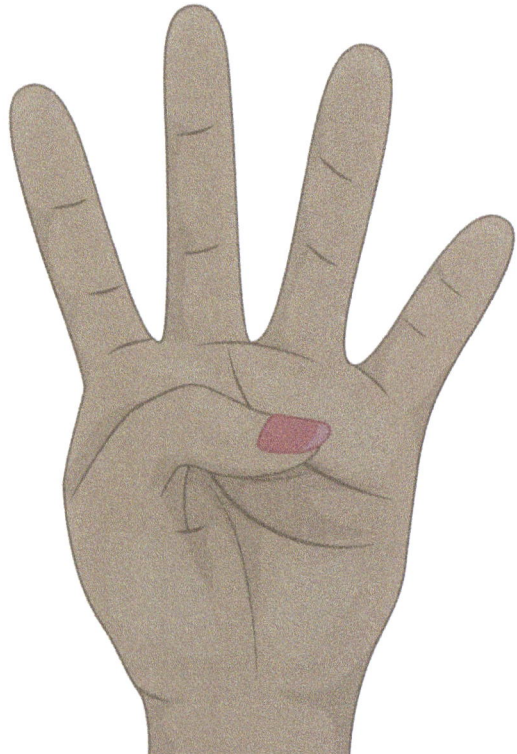

nine

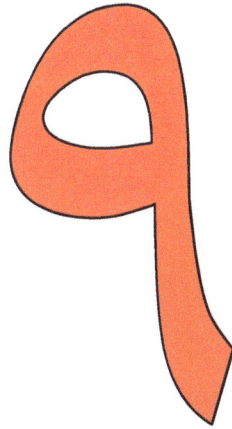

noh

نُه

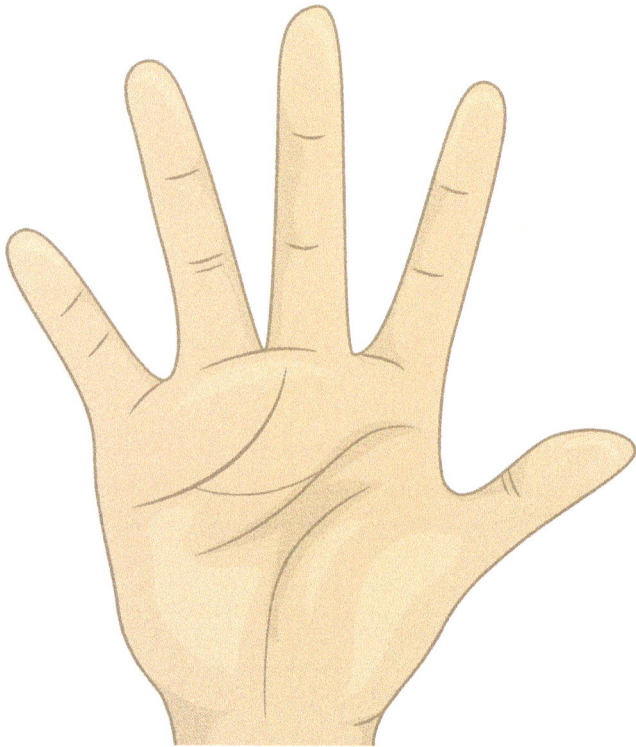 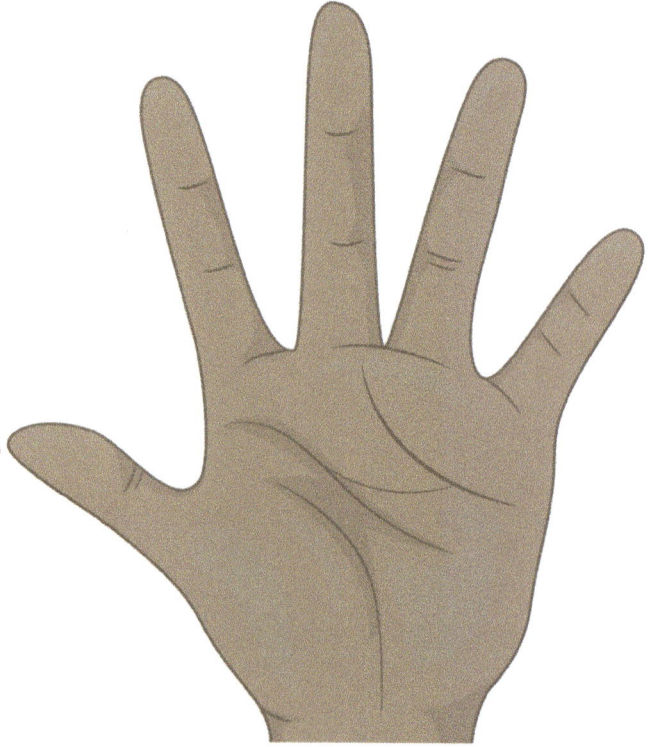

ten

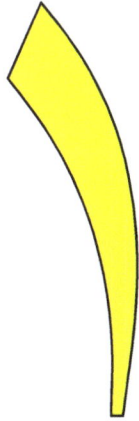 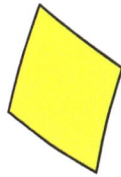

dah

دَه

What is the time?

Sá'at chand ast?

ساعَت چَند اَست؟

á: as (a) in arm

It is 7 [seven] o'clock

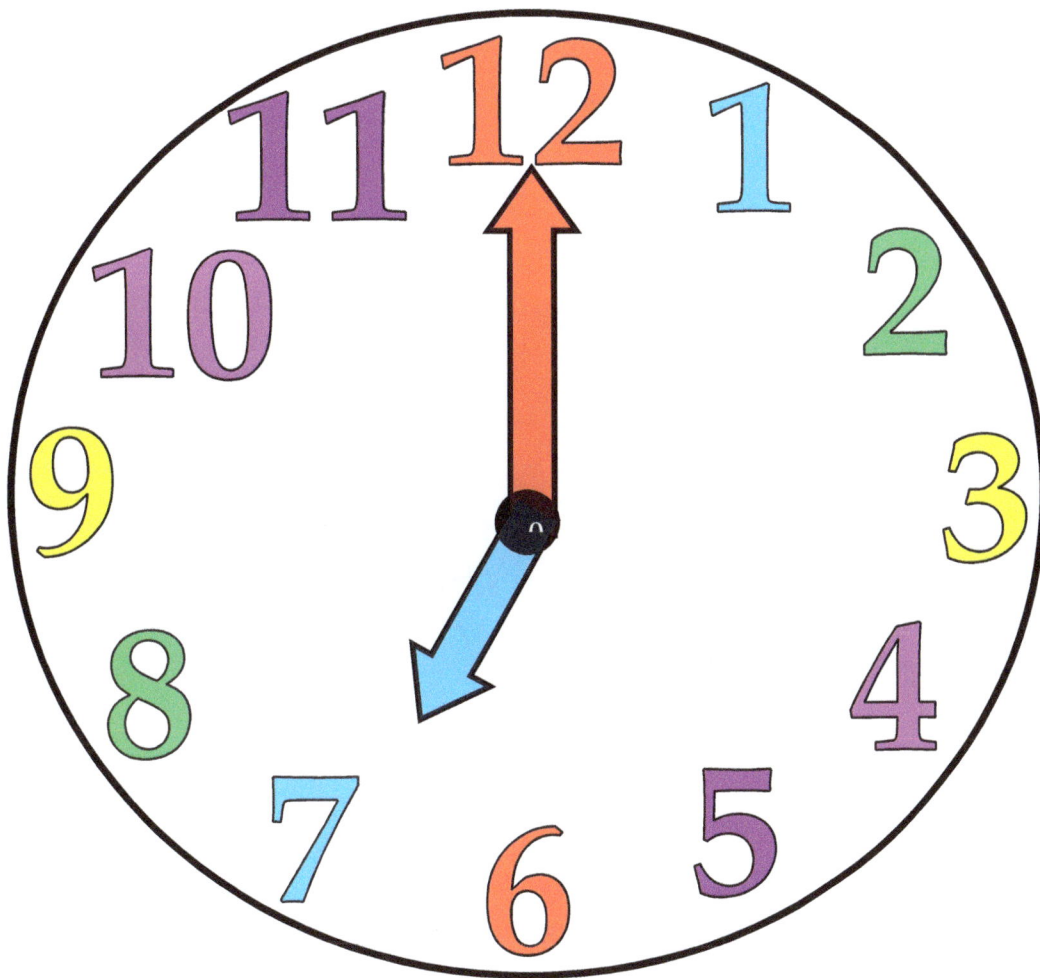

Sá'at ٧ [haft] ast.

ساعَت هَفت اَست

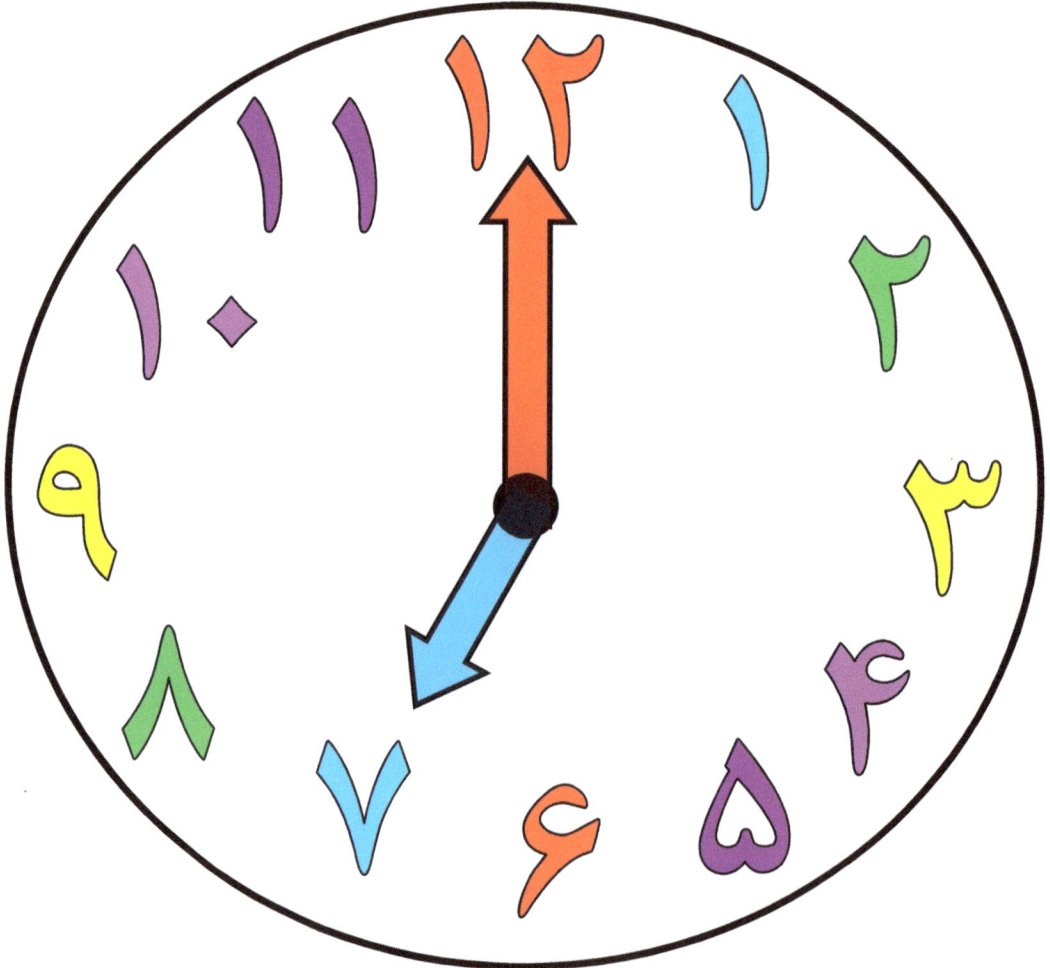

á: as (a) in arm

'**ghrabeh bozorg**
Big hand
عَقرَبِه بُزرک

clock
sá'at
ساعَت

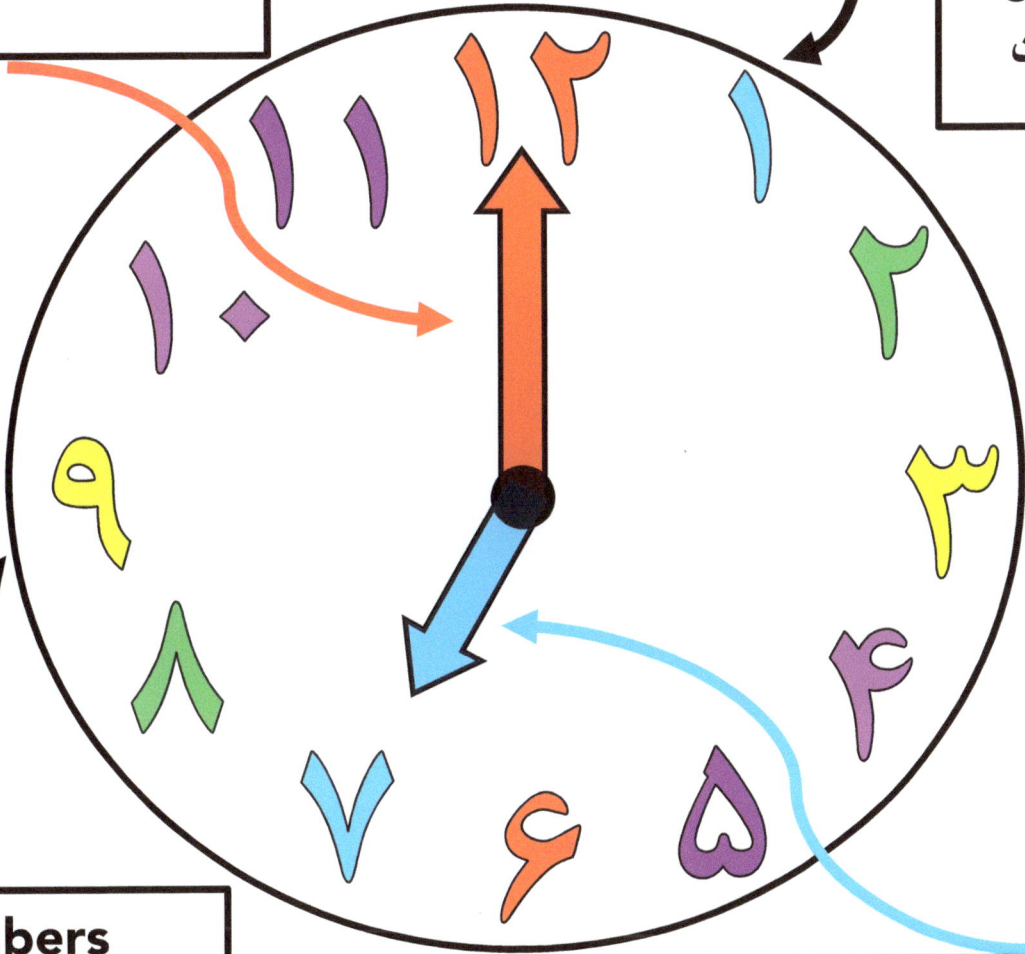

Numbers
Shomáreh
شُماره

A'ghrabeh kúchak
Small hand
عَقرَبِه کوچَک

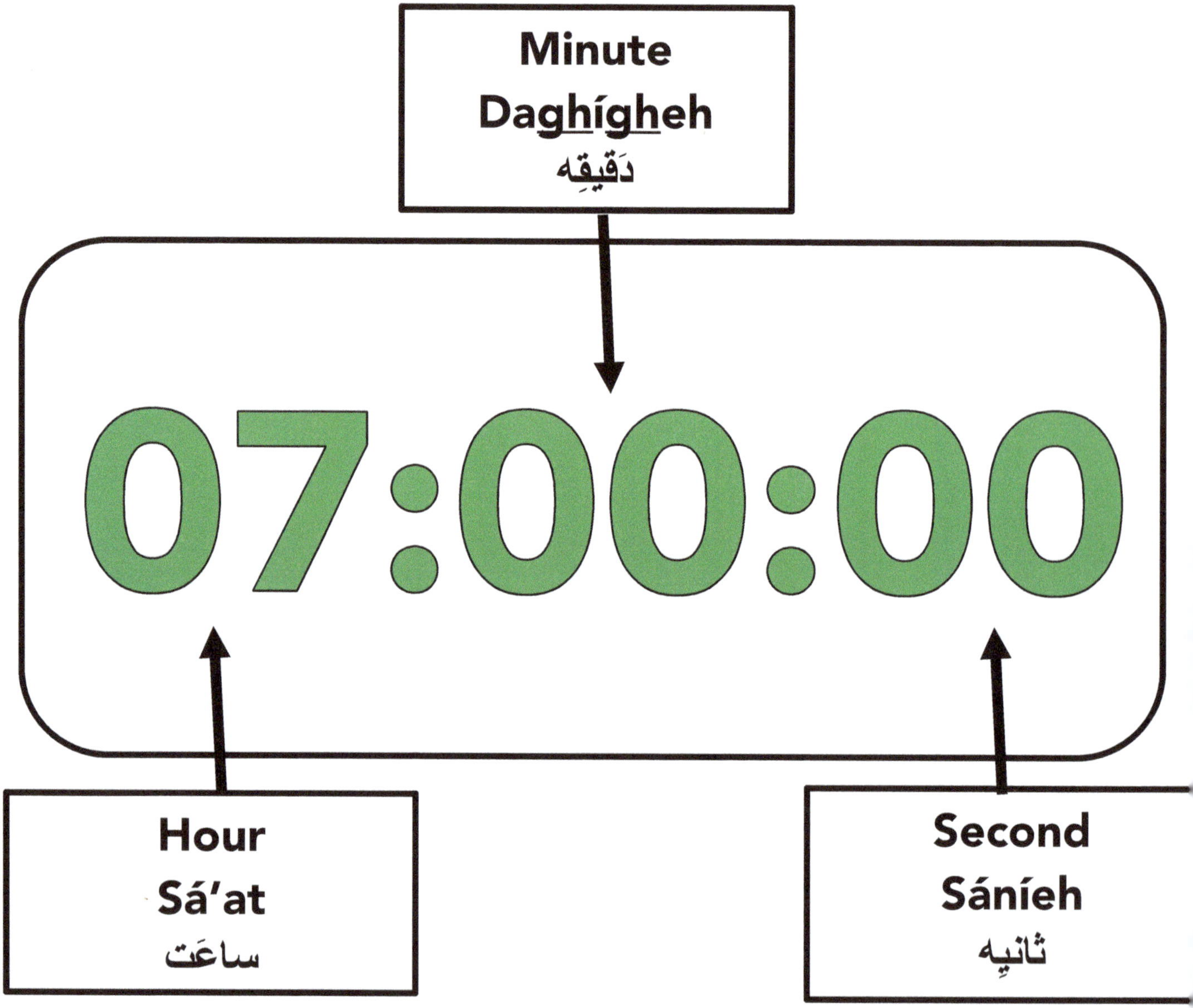

Minute
Daghígheh
دَقیقه

07:00:00

Hour
Sá'at
ساعَت

Second
Sáníeh
ثانیه

Maths

Ríází

رياضى

í: as (ee) in m<u>ee</u>t
á: as (a) in <u>a</u>rm

plus/addition

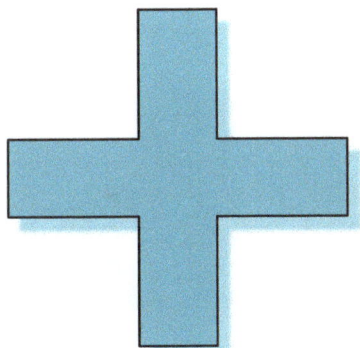

jam' kardan

جَمع کردَن

(ezáfeh kardan / ezáfeí)

minus/take away from

menhá

مِنـها

(manfí / tafrígh)

á: as (a) in <u>a</u>rm
í: as (ee) in m<u>ee</u>t

divide by

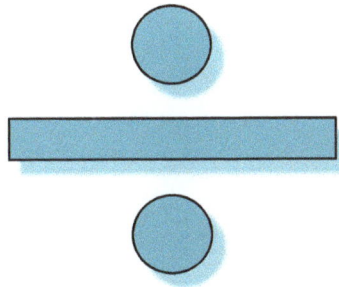

taghsím kardan

تَقسیم کردَن

í: as (ee) in meet

multiply by

zarb kardan

ضَرب کردَن

equal

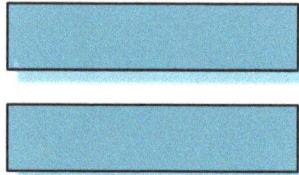

mosáví

مُساوى

(barábar)

á: as (a) in <u>a</u>rm
í: as (ee) in m<u>ee</u>t

weight

vazn

وَزن

Quick Reference: Numbers

English	Finglisi™	Persian
one	yek	یِک
two	do	دو
three	seh	سه
four	chahár	چَهار
five	panj	پَنج
six	shesh	شِش
seven	haft	هَفت
eight	hasht	هَشت
nine	noh	نُه
ten	dah	دَه
eleven	yázdah	یازدَه
twelve	davázdah	دَوازدَه
thirteen	sízdah	سیزدَه
fourteen	chahárdah	چَهاردَه
fifteen	pánzdah	پانزدَه
sixteen	shánzdah	شانزدَه

Quick Reference: Numbers & Time

English	Finglisi™	Persian
one hundred	yek sad	یِک صَد
one thousand	yek hezár	یِک هِزار
second	sáníeh	ثانیه
minute	daghígheh	دَقیقه
hour	sá'at	ساعَت
clock	sá'ate dívárí	ساعَتِ دیواری
watch	sá'ate mochí	ساعَتِ مُچی
time	vaght	وَقت
numbers	shomáreh	شُماره
watch	sá'at	ساعَت
first	aval[ín]	اَوَلین
second	dovom[ín]	دُوُمین
third	sevom[ín]	سِوُمین
fourth	chahárom[ín]	چَهارُمین
fifth	panjom[ín]	پَنجُمین
sixth	sheshom[ín]	شِشُمین
tenth	dahom[ín]	دَهُمین

Quick Reference: Maths

English	Finglisi™	Persian
maths	ríází	ریاضی
to calculate	hesáb kardan	حِساب کردَن
plus/addition	jam' kardan	جَمع کردَن
minus	menhá	مِنها
divide by	taghsím kardan	تَقسیم کردَن
multiply by	zarb kardan	ضَرب کردَن
equal	vaght	مُساوی
weight	vazn	وَزن
English	Englísí	اِنگلیسی
Persian	Fársí	فارسی

www.ingramcontent.com/pod-product-compliance
Lightning Source LLC
Chambersburg PA
CBHW040245100426
42811CB00011B/1161